Since 1975, El Arroyo has been serving up Tex-Mex with a side of laughs on our famous marquee sign that stands on the corner of West 5th and Campbell in Austin, Texas. The Last Queso Stop Before a Bunch of Yoga Studios - over the years we've covered every food pun imaginable while never forgetting witty commentary on current events. The face(s) behind the daily marquee messages remains a secret for now... But we're always happy to take submissions from customers and internet fans. Thanks to you, the buyer of this book, and all of our followers - thanks for smiling. We hope to bring you years of smiles to come!

Cheers,
El Arroyo

2

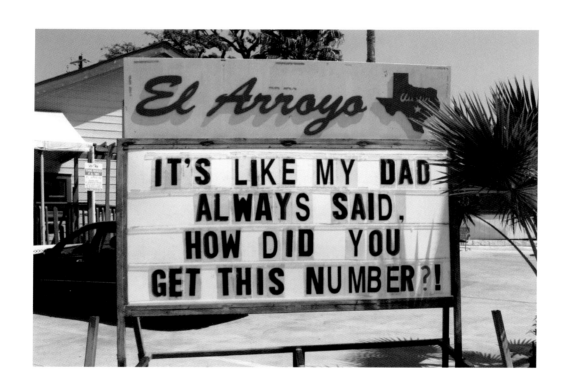

24

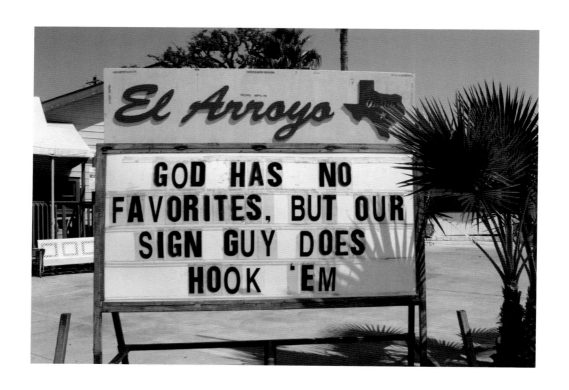

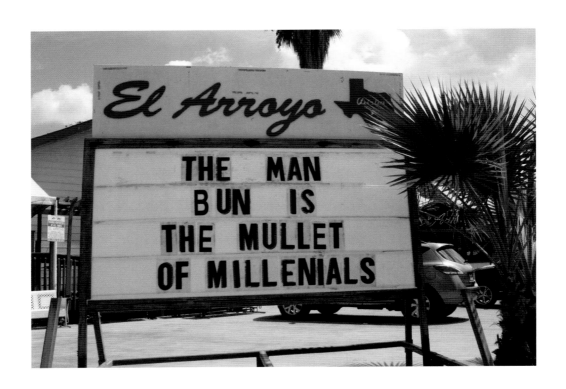

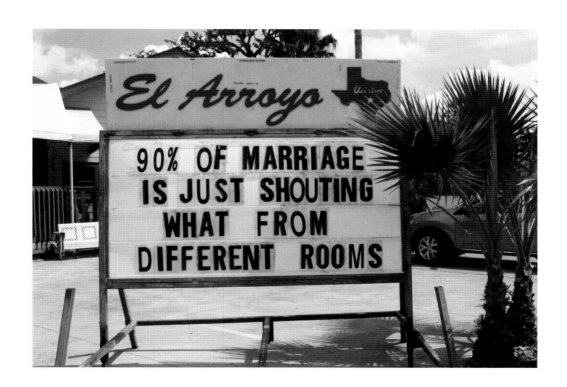

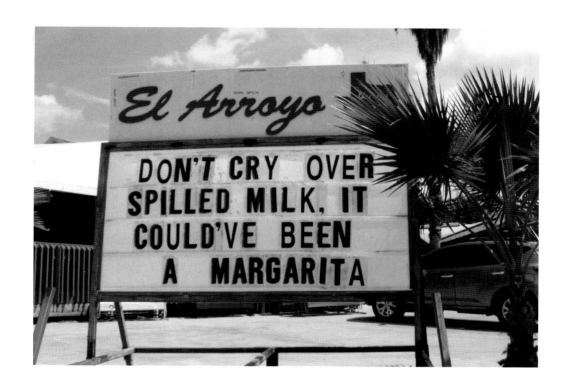

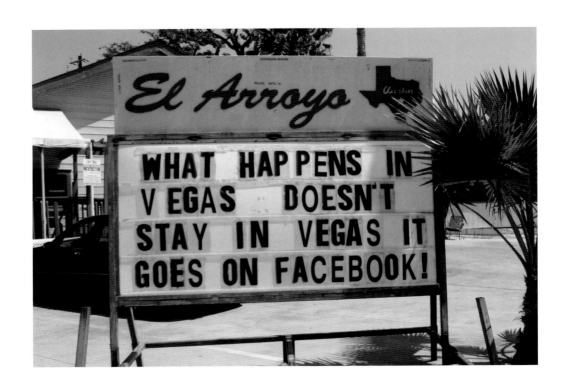

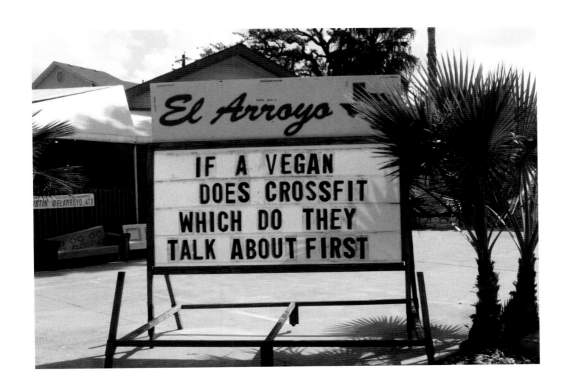

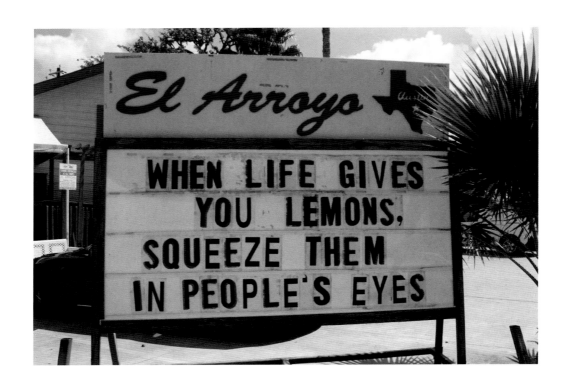

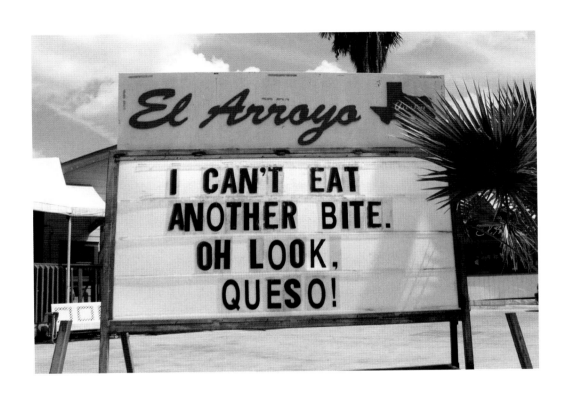

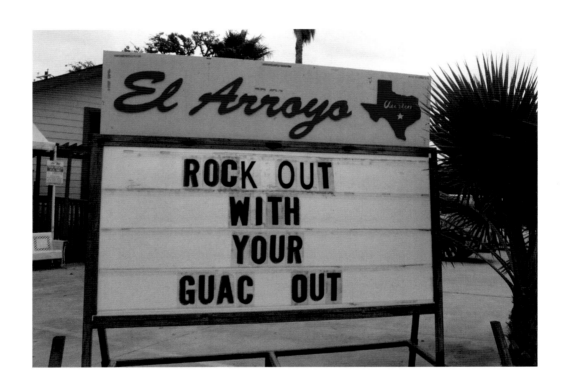

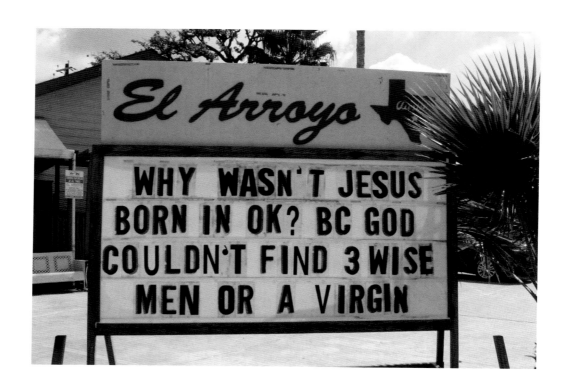

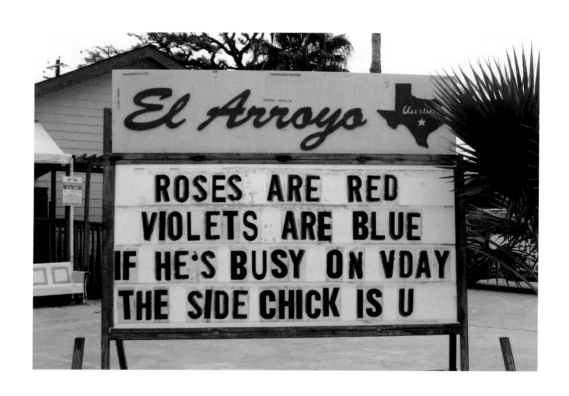

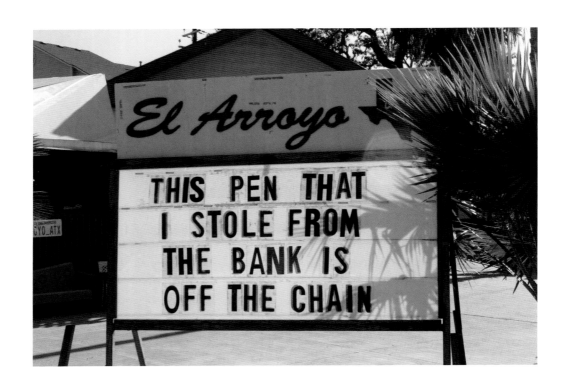

El Arroyo

THE PAST, THE PRESENT
AND THE FUTURE
WALKED INTO A BAR
IT WAS TENSE

126

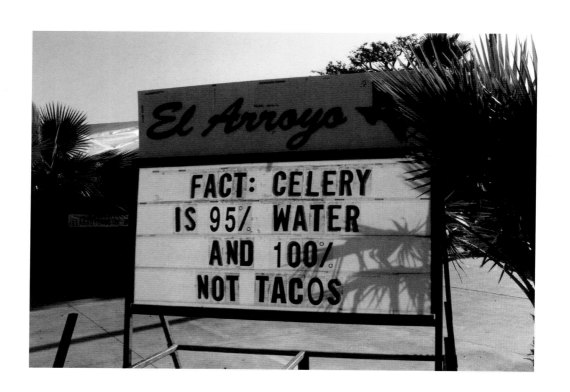

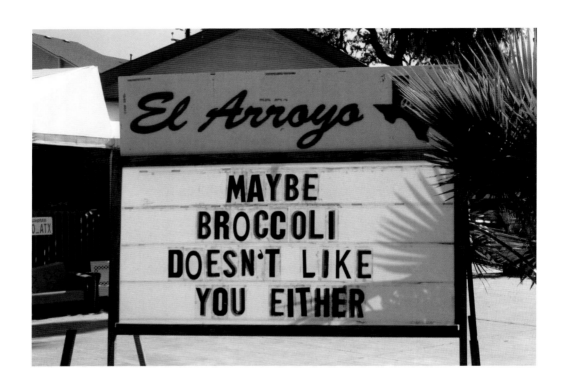

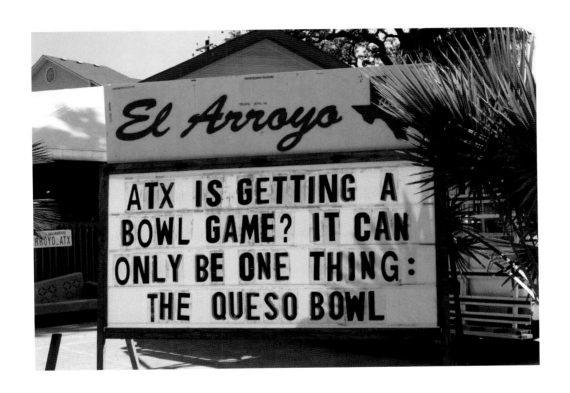

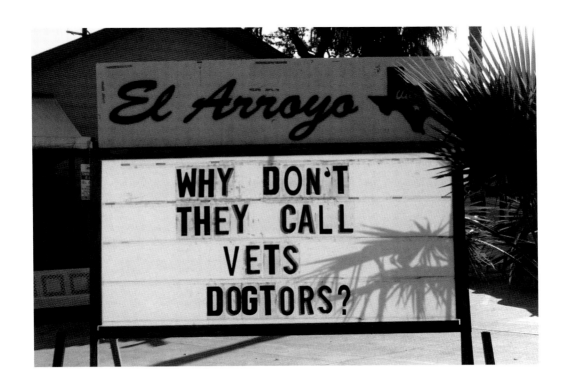

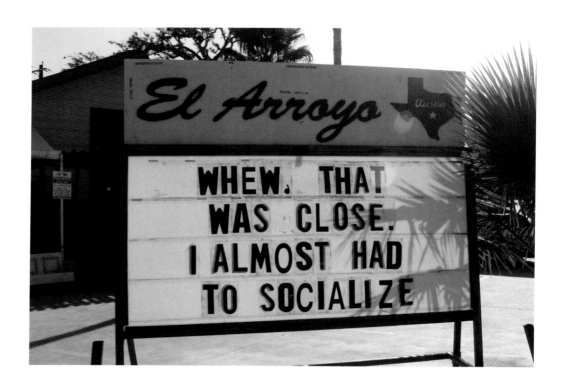

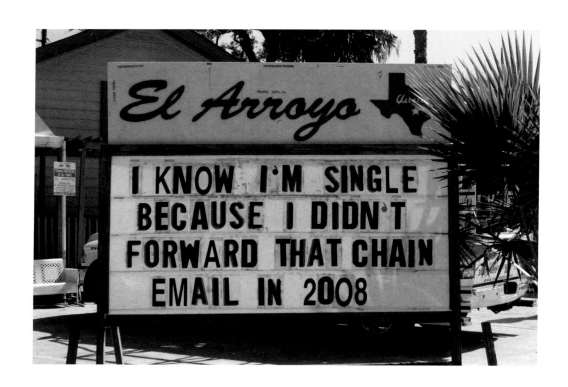

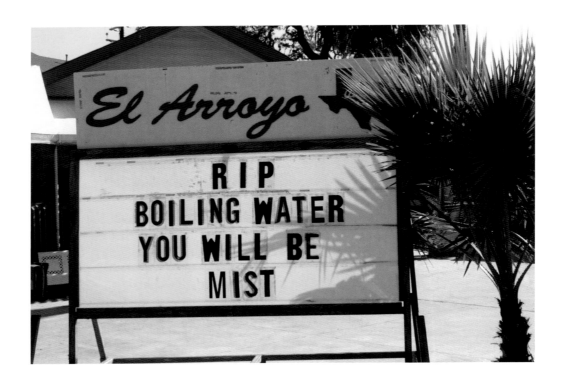

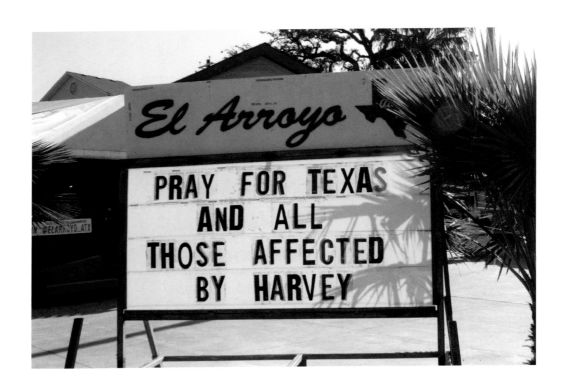

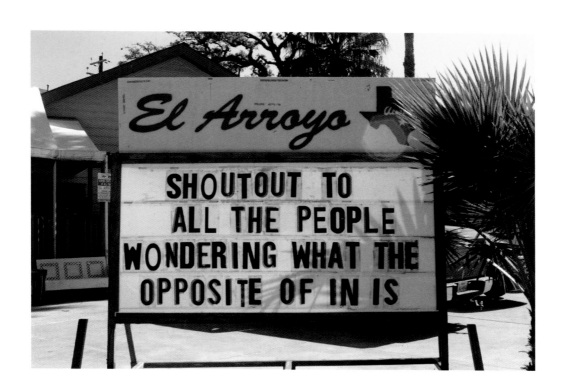

ISBN 978-0-692-97930-3

Library of Congress Control Number: 2017961203

Some characters and events in this book are fictitious. Any similarity to real persons, living or dead, is coincidental and not intended by the author.

Editing by Paige Winstanley
Front cover image by Paige Winstanley
All photographs by Cozumel Publishing Company, LLC
Book design by Hannah Fenves

Printed and bound in the USA
First Printing November 2017

Published by Cozumel Publishing Company, LLC
P.O. Box 50550
Austin, TX, USA 78763
Visit www.elarroyo.com